Captivity

Captivity

LAURIE SHECK

· · · *Alfred A. Knopf   New York*   2007   · · ·

THIS IS A BORZOI BOOK
PUBLISHED BY ALFRED A. KNOPF

www.aaknopf.com

Grateful acknowledgment is made to the following for permission to reprint previously published material:

Harvard University Press: Excerpt from *The Letters of Emily Dickinson,* edited by Thomas H. Johnson (Cambridge, Massachusetts: The Belknap Press of Harvard University Press). Copyright © 1958, 1986 by the President and Fellows of Harvard College. Copyright © 1914, 1924, 1932, 1942 by Martha Dickinson Bianchi. Copyright © 1952 by Alfred Leete Hampson. Copyright © 1960 by Mary L. Hampson. Reprinted by permission of Harvard University Press.

Harvard University Press and the Trustees of Amherst College: Excerpts from "Experiment escorts us last" and "No rack can torture me" from *The Poems of Emily Dickinson,* edited by Thomas H. Johnson (Cambridge, Massachusetts: The Belknap Press of Harvard University Press). Copyright © 1951, 1955, 1979, 1983 by the President and Fellows of Harvard College. Reprinted by permission of Harvard University Press and the Trustees of Amherst College.

New Directions Publishing Corp.: Excerpt from "Sappho: Fragment #24" from *7 Greeks* by Guy Davenport. Copyright © 1995 by New Directions Publishing Corp. Reprinted by permission of New Directions Publishing Corp.

Library of Congress Cataloging-in-Publication Data
Sheck, Laurie.
Captivity / Laurie Sheck.—1st ed.
p. cm.
ISBN-13: 978-0-307-26539-5
I. Title.
PS3569.H3917C37 2007
811'.54—dc22   2006026935

Manufactured in the United States of America
First Edition

J.L.P.

In sickness and in health

Captivity is Consciousness—
So's Liberty.

—Emily Dickinson,
from Poem #384

"We thank thee Oh Father" for these strange Minds, that enamor us against thee.

—Emily Dickinson
in a letter to Mrs. T. W. Higginson,
LATE SUMMER 1876

. . . chance left free to act falls into an order as well as purpose.

—Gerard Manley Hopkins,
from his journal,
FEBRUARY 24, 1873

Contents

Captivity

This homesickness of mind
    Like cuts made almost tenderly in flesh. The surfaces of things grown slow and
Dangerous
    Beneath the desire to apprehend. September light I cannot hear your quiet.
So much elsewhere unsettling each surface, so much annulled.

White sky and such intervals of quiet.
    How even the most still-seeming thing rushes through itself and isn't final.
Particles. Waves. Nor can I compute the possible.
    In my most careful calculations, I am the automaton holding out her bells,
Raising and lowering her fists to a measured, steady ticking. But there is a cast-apart
    In me that marks no hour, and its hands hold no bells at all,

The seconds slant and coarse with split-asunder.

The others hiding away when they took her.

Eventually I learned other words. Assere for knives. Toras: North. Satewa: alone.

Always a breakdown of systems that will not be restored.

Something cuts itself in me. It's not a question of refusal.

Esteronde: to rain. Tesenochte: I do not know.

The shattered of, and then the narrowness opening where the vanished touches it—

Then how the mind recombines and overthrows—

Thinking has a quiet skin. But I feel the *break* and *fled* of things inside it,
    Blue hills most gentle in calm light, then stretches of assail
And ransack. Such tangles of charred wreckage, shrapnel-bits
    Singling and singeing where they fall. I feel the stumbling gait of what I am,
The quiet uproar of undone, how to be hidden is a tempting, violent thing—
    Each thought breaking always in another,

All the unlawful elsewheres rushing in.

The morning's raw and wet.
    There's something delicate and fierce that comes damagingly out of the mind
When the body's ill. I feel the invisible boundaries of my life strike into me
    From regions I can't see, as when red sky assails itself
After intervals of blue, whiteshine, dullish gray. I sense crimson strokes at the edges of things

And have burnt inside myself so many words in a bonfire
    Unseeable but real as dirt. The worst fault a thing can have is unreality.
Here is a window, here a chair. The air swirls with severity and
    Hazard. The chair is white-painted pine, peeling in places, and carved with a five-petalled flower.

Frost, then ridged snow.
    The body can't rest when it's in pain. Outside: hills closed as the cells' glass secrecies,
Waste spaces etched and fissured with genetic script.
    Why should their meanings be clear? Such bold disconsolates
In them, and the tendings, the dividings. The mind would pierce them,
    Being scared. Now on my arm, chopped angled shadows;
And how they enter the eye with their sense of breakage, their sense of outlaw

And estrange.

I'm now in careful hands; I have some fever.
   Something striking sideways and unlooked-for pierces yet this may be so delicate.
Before falling ill I saw elms in small leaf, purple orchis, cowslips, streaks
   Of brilliant electrum. An extremity of mind concealed grows anxious to
Become. The present fury is ash. Still, note

The water coming through a lock. Note green wheat. It's lucent. Perhaps
   It has a chrysoprase bloom.

Was taken by. And the rest scattered. Extremity
   Planting itself in me until I am most Northerly and lost—all tundra-cold whiteness and mistrust.
Winter-taught, ignorant, unsolved.

Daylight in its first and narrowest pulses. Reddish sky.
   This noiselessness in mind-space. What does astray look like, and what is the sound of capture,
The sound of breaking free? Her footsteps moving off into snow-deeps and never-to-come.
   The never-returned of her, smoke from a way station burned down.
And thus she continued. And thus in mind's secret, and in so bitter a cold.

All the more rare and wilder
    In storms of otherwise and then again fettered,
I feel my mind disfiguring itself as if it could not in any other way approach
    The withering, the *frightened back* of things, the buoyancy crushed. Today the fasting girl

Died. Four nurses were sent to watch over her
    But couldn't cross to where she had installed within herself the darkest field.
Like someone watching trees, they couldn't turn with her turnings. I wonder at that country
    She belonged to, the obligation of not, the eye-blur restlessly steering. It's December,

Almost dark at 3:00. They moistened her lips with water as the redness left,
    The skin of a white tiger. She had an air of the knights of chess about her.
Something bitter distills where we can't see.
    It is hard to seize what is.

December night. The north winds shift above the icy hill;
    How they move like an unfinished sentence always, wave-like and varying,
And I think they are beautiful this way, where nothing can explain,
    And the green of the near lies altered and effaced by snow.

This *now* has little of its own—the winds inside it from far off
    Where once the trees had leaves. I don't want to be warm. I don't want a marble
Calm. Branches click like hair triggers, and the ground refuses ownership,
    Each hidden liberty soundless, undisclosed.

I stayed behind, unable to sense any center to things anymore.

    Yet how oddly lawful in itself it seemed and sometimes graceful—

That place in me like water clouded-over or the blanked gray of a computer screen candescing.

    The way it wouldn't break itself, nor allow any thinnings or openings,

An ancient kingdom risen whole and ruthless from the sea.

    I was its Emperor, irrelevant, deposed.

So often in the eyes a shocked tenderness. But where does it go, over

    That gray water, that gray land?

Swamps and thickets. Nothing but tree bark and pieces of old beaver skin to eat.
    How the mind is changed by its thorned removes, its hungers,
The way illness, experimenting on the body, forces it into a *next* it wouldn't have otherwise
    Stumbled toward or known. What is a safe return? What is it to carry an I?
Thoughts break from themselves, odd and brittle.
    Thus did we travel for twenty-six days and as of yet no word of ransom.
Our captors are very kind to one another. I remember an elsewhere of not doubting, but it is far away.

November dissolves itself and so haunts the mind,
    All the tender peripheries theft-ridden, altering, unsolved.
I feel the slow slave trade of my eyes, their harsh collecting, though every calculation
    Ends in broken. Expeditions. Savageries.

The shadows in the flesh are very strong.

But to whom can I say *I am thy creature?*
   The minute bafflements build like a slow fever, the way shock converses with itself
Until it becomes its own rampant landscape, half-tranquilized and burnt
   With mourning. And the quietness so brittle, as if starved.
This strange liberty, this thinnest of shelters—I feel it explode itself always. This tossed-back
   Into no answer, each hard storm of

Partial and endure—

No clockwork prayer

For I can find no clockwork prayer in me. How the near-enough never resolves itself,
    Only carries such clefts of *else* and *never* as it goes,
Strict cliffs where the mind breaks itself on itself. Volatile
    Thou who is not Thou,
Other I am in the world and far. O broker,
    Trust rushes so suddenly away. Each shock ignites

A contradiction. In this wild ungentle a soft pulsing
    Quickens oddly. How truthful the ruins which so partially disclose.

More distinctive than the smell of walnutleaf or camphor
    This severity, this faltering self-hewn and grievous.
Today a shocking thing: a young man put out his eyes.
    Being medically trained, he must have known how to proceed, yet it was barbarously
Done with a stick and some wire.
    The eyes were found among the nettles in the field.
He won't say what was the reason.

We live in accumulations of the actual
    With so little understanding. Neither am I very strong now.

How alien, how chilling, this austere and fierce machinery of thinking.

The way sunlight amends
    The eyes, too, grow practiced in unsteadiness and fracture.
I write this to you on air as I walk, but I think now all summary is betrayal.
    I picture your hands lifting a fork or folding cloth, while at the same time
I'm thinking, *it was believed if their cornfields were cut down they would starve and die with hunger,*
    And *was missing from* and *could learn no tidings . . .* And *they who have taken me*

Were driven from the little they had . . . he fetched me some water and told me
    I could wash. All these so braided, where hurt is building nimbly.
I feel a pleasure of *never contained* sweep over me, now that I know place is never
    Clear or wholly settled, not even the veins on the underside of a leaf, its freedoms.
Crossing is a hard simple. The feet register the merest intervals and shifts;
    All that is tracked is also otherwise and hidden.

Waking I saw chains of light on the wall—
    Most curious to me the visible world in that it has no motive,
Its structures richly growing or diminishing, regular or irregular, converging or diverging,
    Whereas I stumble down steep stairs
Looking for an equal sign a theorem worn keys to a dark that speaks most confused then blue
    And soon scattering.

May in bloom. Irises blooming.
    This time of year's a hand opened from the wrist, and reaching.

This fragility of things
    When the sun goes down and the trees are X-rays,
Nerve-patterns stilling in synapses, cold folds. Tenderness stalks these granite
    Hills, as if scrutiny could ransom what it covets.
Chaos steps quietly here; no voice-over with it, no scar.

. . .

No voice-over running, no scar
    On these long fields night's sheared and emptied of their brokenness,
Clefts, small warrings hidden.

If I could see into a human genome I'd see long spaces much like this,
    Vast stretches of empty surfaces, then clusters of information teeming,
Then still more empty stretches—

As tonight, reading, I see the spaces between brackets
    Where the words of the ancients have been lost—

```
[                      ]
[     ] that labor [            ]
[     ] to sing [            ]
[       ] a storm wind [          ]
[       ] and no pain [          ]
```

What survives is mutilated, torn—on scraps of papyrus
   Used to mummify crocodiles, on pottery shards.
It's the brackets that I've grown to love; how they don't banish the lostness
   But give voice and space to absence, blanks.

As now, the curtains pulsing over the open window
   Make of it a lost, unsettled place
Between the solid fields of wall.

. . .

When I felt my mind tear, words flared in it like electric light, like currents buzzing.
   It had brackets in it surrounding things I couldn't see
And the brackets were locked gates
   At each end of a field I couldn't enter. Some days there were many such fields,

On other days just few. The brackets were rigid, of a silvery quality,
   Surrounded by a redblack air.
A bracket will not allow dissection.

I peered through them to the space I couldn't enter. Quiet field without possession.
   No scar-trace or word-trace I could see.

. . .

If I closed my book in the lamplight (the others sleeping, the rough sound of their breathing)
   Would I find the poem of my nightblack field,
And would it look like this?—
[   ]
                        the wayfarer

silent hidden
                        [*indecipherable*]
                        unreachable
[   ]
what loves.

. . .

In the newspaper the diagram of the human genome
    Looked true the way photos of the moon look true, the way drawings of neurons,
All flaying, reaching tentacles and readiness seem true. So much busyness
    And struggle, then nothing for a while, then the intense
Attentiveness, elemental, a body needs to become for a time unvanishing,
    Repeating itself through the world.

This is what's inside of us, I thought. How strange, this landscape of *inside*.

Still, such lost places in my mind when I think of it—
                       [*indecipherable*]
                       unreachable
[   ]
[   ] what
loves.

Sometimes a bare peace, a restoration.
    Too much veil in me, she thinks, if otherness is to sift further in,
And must sift further in. Reason is a fragile wing.
    But I must cross and cross over even so. Far into otherwise and fractured,
The irreconcilable estrangement of me breaking.
    Why must the mind cover itself why hide itself why bind itself in quiet and in dark—

And became very cold, coiled back,

    The articulations vanishing. Inside me a bold stretch of blue scattering away,

Then burnt white.

    What is this chain of feelings by which we mean (if it is that) a self?

A thing of more or less opacity, depending. Still, I've seen a red that does not mean,

    I've seen blue shadow, and structures most definite in their carvings

As if no further correctness could be wished them.

    For every cliff and limb and edge

Skeined in the afternoon and threatening

    There is a rinsing tenderness, and I am held here, and so met and accidented

By perhaps.

Many thanks for your letter.
    The other day we were given vaccinations, but one of us already stood apart,
His entire face and arms marked by the smallpox, and on his neck a star-clump like singed
    Nerves, or spidery white kisses. Seeing him, I felt something strike at me, inside me, impale its
Chisel there, unlike the winged recoil of the violet's leaves.
    And then the earthline wavered, a grimace briefly shadowsharp and fractured.

Bitter north wind, hail and sleet. I grow flexible and mingled.
    Shock brings with it a silent conviction of wonder.

Comfort binds itself

Thinking is a truceless act.
    How it holds the injured *yets* and *thens* inside it, so many layers of barter
And resist. You who are all swerve,
    Distance and blindfold when I try to find you—

Why did you plant in us, within our very cells,
    Such stinging cuts and tense pleasures born of wars; each chaotic
Torn-away and knotted freedom?
    Comfort binds itself restless and apart:
The *yes* disfigured, then the power of its tracing flame.

For I have missed the feeling of being able to go somewhere else,
    Delicately barred as I am
In this slow conversion of myself into nothingness—
    It's as if all that visits the mind
Is a great fire on an altar but I stand before it and am cold. I watch rich folds

Of sky and feel how my eyes fail, trying to adjust, take hold—there are after-images, astigmatism,
    Irradiation, such movements of accommodation and convergence
As I can barely comprehend, yet they are mine. Through this glare of self-distrust and longing
    I sense in the distance a crisp whiteness
But it's roughed overall with my wrong articulations, apprehensions,
    And so is darked.

Fog gowning the hill, then slashed to burning.
    Into this far and barely-marked inside my mind I seek you, protector,
But you are quiet, undisclosed. I feel the kind topography of wind, its shapes
    Cool and inhuman. Want them ever closer.
Have you broken apart in your far-from-here, your always-absence, have you
    Shattered to burnt galaxies of atoms? How does one call to that which is not?—Yet even so—

Rope-burn

Maybe there is in silence a remoter tenderness,
    Uncharted peace most delicate and threatened. But I feel the rope-burn's dizzying mystery on me
Always, the long scald of it pressing on the captive's wrists. Such parched riverbeds
    It carves there, such raw breakage of suppose and comfort.
How can the mind caught up in fright not harm itself, not dream the killing-parties
    Ever? Not be lost in this thick wilderness of branchings
Where it feels the brutal *never,*

Stinging bond.

Did not foresee

The mind is a thing deeply marked. I have bound myself to this damage.
  Most delicate and difficult
Strangeness, I have abandoned the idea of being
  Warm. There's a strictness in the ice charged with its distinct breakages,
Hard and beautifully detached—water once so blue polished to a sheen until it's heightened
  And unlike itself.

Outside, cold hills. The sky steel-colored, then duller in parts, the gray of smudged newsprint.
  I did not foresee
How this becoming is a reckless and incautious thing. The ice
  Grows intricate where the stresses fall.

And no summer as yet, but it will come with its bright pieces of whatever,
    Sorted by the eye yet still uncaptured,
Greenly branched and various with promise. I'd like to watch it long enough,
    Held fast by the laws of its sequencings and shapings, and be so carried, the way the mind goes in
Search of an *after* that will temper what has come before,

Or sometimes not—: Did I tell you of the man I visited last week, who hasn't lost the ability
    To move his tongue, his lips, to laugh or cry or sing or use his voice, yet is unable
To utter any words, just a few unintelligible syllables,
    And recognizing this, stares into the fact of it
As at the eggs in an opened anthill? I don't know how to think of him. We are so rawly made,
    So carried into the harsh and almost-dark.

As if stung in the throat. As if seared by a narrow wire-like blaze
    Sharply upon the air and always.

For there is so much crumbling and instead. I think of you now writing that last
    Note. How the *apart*s multiply, grow wild with clash and scatter. Or resolve into a calm
I can barely understand—a wasp's nest, maybe, the papery regularity of its cells,
    All those steady *carefuls* lining up. Your thin, your brittle wrist, gave back

Its weight, its mass, its shadow—but to what? And now, in me, the far of your death
    Sternly whitens the notion of *to see*. You, now, not singular, but interspersed
Among the questions,

Elsewheres of water rushing down stone steps.

But how each thought hacks and scalds itself
    As if there were no settlement to return to anymore,
Jealous of the sweeping rain and in night-season cold under it.
    I went on foot and careless. She, who once was traded for a gun. She, led away into Removes.
The cut thread of her, the *and with bitterness I carried* . . . And then nothing but wilderness,
    And being taken by, and a sorrow that cannot.

No purchase

I've come far North.
    The ice insists like a vast inexplicable tenderness of being, or an inquiry
For which there is no answer. This white far has no purchase but itself,
    Ignites itself plainly. Doesn't think *what boundaries of* or *lacking food or shelter.*
Doesn't think, *What claim, what passage through, what profit, what contract, what frenzy of dissection.*
    The brutal unsolved is a stark liberty.
Matter has no ideal to pursue. I drift out from the sole inlet of *to know.*

Now December strikes in with its own brittleness, as when an otherwise
    Opens in the body, wrenching further into slant and hazard.
Past the covert operations of the state, past checkpoints and official access,
    A crystal splits along the lines of its own cleavage.
Questions unshelter themselves harshly. Each war-zone of them flaring, and radical with damage.

But *suppose* is very fragile and away.
    Now, among the oaks and walnut trees, threat builds in me a tenser, riven place.
I feel it press against my ribs, the steeps in it and thievery; what's gentle crumbles
    Into guardedness and shards. Our provisions now are groundnuts, acorns, purslane, weeds.
Hunger's made of me a spy of comfort. For I have passed very quickly from *to own*.

Trees bending, shockwaves of mind. Tender maelstroms
    Of astray and sunder. And shudderings of late summer light on the hill
As when hurt pathways of thought
    Become habitable scars, strange comfort of roughness, hectic-calm.
No captions beneath them, no marketing director saying, "Our job is to make people
    Buy things they don't need or want."

How secretive the brain is. So many banishments inside it, so much sting.
    I watch the leaf-darks sway among the lit ones,
Cureless in their turnings, flicks of wind.

But there are so many thresholds in the body.
    The cells in their distant otherness inside me. As if I stood beside them blinded,
Their script unbrailled, an iron away in them, a veiling,
    As when computer files won't open though they're called up by their codes,
A glitch in the system keeping them separate and unknown.
    There is no clarifying edge.
Watchfulness is a weak captive of itself.

All the fiercer and lawlessly irregular
　　These intervals of withdrawal where I am a burned field
And above me the sky is thickening and clouding.
　　In that field, little Stonehenge of the heart
Mysteriously standing, its distinct construction odd and uninjured in this yellow
　　Light. If I say I was flexible, was harmed, was cleansed, was helped, was deeply marked,
I still can't understand what I have been. Doubt falls in me falls through me
　　A rough and intricate hazard. The mind carries an austere
Inwardness that will not put out its eyes.

Every day in another language.

    As when we passed the hill where one of their villages once prospered.

Not of tents, but of wooden houses arranged in a manner of streets much like our own.

    Many had perished there of smallpox.

An *apart* pierces and yet at times I cross a dark most near them. I've been a long time now

    From walls, that grip of certain.

There are such vanishings inside each quiet. So many plurals and veerings, so much away—

And then inwardly each question presses hard
    Against the curious hollows and the sharp *and yet*s. It's what I felt that first
Frigid winter when the early carefulness

Crumbled (that new land)—and then the long afterwards began—
    Of snow mounding on the overhangs of roofs pocked as waxen cells
Imprinted with the marks of bees' jaws. And the questions rising in me, too,
    Were those rough marks, precise irregularities
From which I knew I must set out—
    Into the *instead*s, into the odd (and yet I must) and roadless to the eye
And curved and steep and coarse and keenly branching.

I'm sorry not to have written you sooner.
    We are peculiar forms, like someone's old papers rifled quickly through
But not read before the burning.
    How to speak of the icy cave-like place I lately feel,
Its white reluctance dividing me from all things I desire and see.
    I think it must often be the case
That one holds within oneself a guardedness, expectant, steeply quarried,
    The way mistakes grow magnified inside the mind, spiked and sharply gleaming.

How skilled, how dominant, this white unswaying place.
    And I wonder how, bred from our churning, it constructs itself so strongly
Like the crush of light I sometimes at the noonhour hear.

And then the mind begins to starve itself. As if the brain clefts were giving back their networks,
    All their tensile webs. Unsafe the worldspeed and the scalded
Warnings. Quiet as errors in genetic script
    Or handcuffs left rusting on a table, the folds and softs
Are vanished from the air. Shock knits a ragged fabric. Each move leads into

Ambush and undone.

Morning light unsealing over the river. Widening sky.

    Such an odd species we are that locks itself up, or locks itself in from within.

Wardened and opposed. The eyes are such curious creatures and yet. Tempted, drawing back.

There are now thirty of us sick, and deaths among us daily. May 7th, Sarah Lydle, whose name was Braint

    When she was taken, and who married during this our captivity, died, and on the 13th, Mr. Smead's

        son Daniel

Died, and Christian Tether on the 14th. I am grown very weak. The prison is made of stone and lime.

Hazard wanders over itself, charts and marks its own body. Excisions. Deletions.

    In the sky, so much of further, so much of lost.

Like the fretting of blades closing
  I feel a sense of my own disappearing as it rises inside me. How hot it grows,
Tin-bright then notched like the river in torrent; breaks in the rocks are dark eyes.
  The sky behind me reclines like an Egyptian king,
Gold-edged and final.

Inside has odd ways: so much cutting away
  In the thinking of, in each view intercepted by *instead,* the sharpened bolts
Of looking back. I'm releasing into shadows I can't know. Tall larches by the river
  Become what they can't recover from—leaning over
Into how they are changed, rough and so tender, nearly all.

But what is this mixture of mutiny and stringent peace
    By which I feel, inside myself, the volatile discordance of the world?
October scatters quietness, burns up the veil of this fierce chemistry, this gravity of atoms.
    As if washed by an alien hand
My skin grows colder where the mind no longer binds it,
    And then this thinning and widening as of fever,
And then each eye schooled in tremor and in slash—

Teohare: to be suspended between two different places.
 And yet it seems the remembered home is not one home but clusters
Of otherwise and absence, reeling, ever-changing. Nor is here one single here.
 How the I constantly crumbles yet still stands.
We pass south of the river. I count oak trees, birch trees, beech.

The eye's language brokenness—
    How it depends on 24 frames per second to sustain the impression of continuous
Movement on the screen, sync-pulses scanned and quickly mended.
    Slowed any more the seen world will crack and crevice,
The light become some lawless ragged thing.
    O agile tenderness, I've felt the suddenly-narrow of myself break you

Into flickerings and doubts. The lit screen of me gone wild with shards of never,
    Shockwaves heading like missiles toward what world—

For there are so many forms of opaqueness.
    These sleeper cells plotting and secretive
Inside me beneath the waves of daily tasks etc.
    And this store-voice saying, *How would I know I just work here,*
And *the system's down you'll have to come back later.* Something's being sold to the highest bidder,
    Something's being made to go even faster.

In today's paper: a newly patented device that compares the audio-waves of an infant's
    Cry to a data bank of cries. But
February shreds its stable clarity, and I—
    How frail the *and thens* are. All the wandering, the errant thefts—

Each thought abducts itself into such wilderness—
    So many footsteps away from, footsteps toward,
Herself in separateness unsheltered. Every crossing the feeling of a bone caught in the throat
    Yet wed to a most joyful burning. Her leg wound salved with oak leaves
She heads further toward the promising unsettled, the uncauterized *although*s abiding,
    Leaf-skeins crumbling, tearing.

> *That I might step*

Then I came to a peace so random it felt dangerous.
    Rough battlefield, expectancy, most tenuous and fragile contract,
How can I step with threadbare tenderness
    Across the zero hour of each strike and batter?

Why do we live in time?—its edges crumbling, its contours filling with monuments,
    Hard data. But there is a *very plain* in things that sometimes comes
Just calmly. It holds no trade routes, no borders fortressed, guarded.
    That I may briefly touch it. That I might step into the curious

Despite—

And now this January whiteness destroys the covered-over of itself.

    O warden's hand, I've felt the press and grasp of you; a starved bitterness that answers.

That grating of bone against bone. But look how the ground still holds within each warred-against,

    Each roughness, so many bending threads.

How the *cannot* unbinds itself, though danger colors it always. Exposed is a place

Of plural and begin.

As when the mind separates itself from its extremest places
    Something swerved in me, sealed over. And I must go at their pace, and continue with them
In so biting a cold, the Norths in me hardening, sun stripped of crown.
    Neither are they safe who lead me.
You who paint, if you painted us, we are the spots on the canvas left uncovered.

Locked within alone, still there are way stations.
    I enclose for you a chestnut fan—
Each side of it symmetrical, answering to the other. As if a law runs through it, binding.
    But there's another leaf, the middle one, which belongs to neither one side nor the other.
So I am cryptic to myself, and ignorant. Once I thought if I lay still enough

I might feel a heat press into me
    Until it and I were the same element, or dashes on either side of words
I had forgotten. Matching, unopposed.
    Now, from where I watch, I feel the window, hot with daylight, fill.
Skin has no choice but to converse with the world.

Awkward into worldlight I—
    This stammer of me among woods I walk late summer,
Old logging paths still neatly drawn, pine needles fallen, peat-soft earth,
    Myself all trespass, misunderstanding,
Translating, translating . . .

. . .

Such shifting linkages
    Where the grasses bend. The brain's funerals unfelt inside the soil.
All the questions in it
    Wordless and apart.

If I were veiled if I were shuttered in if I were lily root, unspoken, glacial, unapproachable, undone

If I were trackless, being lost

If I were iron if I were beggar's hand if I were leap and canyon bold slashed sky if I were soil

.   .   .

.Edu.gov.com.mil.org.net.int—
    How well organized it seems,
This net, this netting,
    Terrain of pathways mapped and taken,

Whereas I cannot overthrow this stutter in myself
    As a lily knows by code to be a lily
As the sky carries dangerous ferocities
    Unsettles itself ever
Thrashes against itself—
    Dashes stammerings tumults lightnings waves—

.   .   .

Walked the path late summer patched light on the pastureland before the woods began
I could see through the trees low hills like a delirium of peace such slowness in them and sparrows
Bluejays three wild turkeys running from the sound of me my clumsy feet in the dry leaves the light
Neon-green where sun broke over power lines miles of them built in the summer of '56—

What consoles does wondering console does finding as when he said *I have found now the law of the oak
Leaves. It is of platter-shaped stars altogether; the leaves lie close like pages.* Weeks of walking writing in his
Notebook then *there was no way to shew even whether the flower were shutting or opening*—

. . .

There was no way to shew whether the flower were shutting or opening—

How to know what shuts what opens.
    What consoles does finding console does losing.
This pastureland all curves and openings leading to farther closings and openings,
    While sentences break in me because I am a thing that breaks.

At the precise time of day he watched he couldn't tell
    What the petals were doing, only that a direction was being taken, a process
Set in motion,
    Then the pencil tucked inside the knapsack. Then footsteps again, heading back.

. . .

Unaltered, the deepest errors of me.
    I walk the woods' untamed astrays.
Such quiet uproar abiding.
    Greenshine over all.

To come near but not in is a hardness, a wilderness of far.
    The shadows break but the eye is a stranger to them ever.
The pulse assembles itself deliberately, casting small nets
    Toward the uncertain. But can a mind in red bloom grow rich with threat and enter?
On purpose but not, how it must bend and shake, no longer skilled at fixed
    And banished. Then what does it feel like, that raw entering, that leaving,
Where the end must be different from the beginning?

This confused manner of the dust, of things that mix, must mix,
    As branches extend in wind
Then lash and shudder back, hitting against themselves, gnarled, sun-bitten, cureless, unconfined.
    Or they turn on themselves, a stern scrutiny. Or grow calm
But never wholly still, as when leaves, like sensor-chips, register the slightest mutations of air.

. . .

The man in the asylum—
Did he watch the trees registering wind, dust rising and swirling, settling back?
"For there is a language of flowers."
"For there is a sound reasoning upon all flowers."
"For flowers are musical in ocular harmony."
He walked out to tend the garden plot allowed him,
Then, back inside, continued writing—

O what can words
The weak interpreters of mortal thoughts . . .

Or what can thoughts tho' wild of wing they rove . . .

And, *"Winter of all. Be mindful,"* This he read in Latin.

. . .

Winter has made of these trees black rips against the sky.
   Clouds rush by, a volatile curelessness. I walk on. The hill so steady,
Not shredding itself in this wind.
   So many unsettled openings I can't see. So much crushed beneath
My awkward feet.

Winter of all be mindful.
Wild of wing.

. . .

The wind shifts and then steadies
   But with small breakages the eye can't see.
"I want to forget all I know, I am trying to learn what I do not know . . . the colors that bewilder . . ."
   O what can words, or what can thoughts . . .
Almost all of Smart's letters were burned;
   Only a handful of business correspondence survives, mainly asking for money.
No one saw any reason to keep them, those traces of a man
   Who went from asylum to debtor's prison where he died, praising all things—what falters
And breaks, what's humble and minute and harmed:

"For the mouse is a creature of great personal valour."

. . .

He thought about the letter "l," the Hebrew letter *Lamed,*
    And saw God in this letter.

"For l is the grain of the human heart & on the network of the skin."
"For l is in the veins of all stones both precious and common."
"For l is in the grain of wood."

But I can find no single letter for these rips of mind that thinking is,
    These strivings of mind so like a hand that crumbles at the moment that it touches—
Wild of—winter of all—both precious and common—grain of wood.

. . .

Dust rises from the road,
Ashes of burned letters or the wonderings of mind.
Once a hand moved across the page, but it is dust from a debtor's prison, lost.
Winter of all. Be mindful. Wild of wing.
There must have been thousands of burned letters; one of the few surviving asks
For "wished goodness."

. . .

I think it must be heath-rough, wild, the brain, shocked with its most
    Intricate hesitations, costs.
Where is the language of flowers? Where the node of fear? A pleasure center
    Flickers. But the place that shreds itself in blackness, the place that wants
More veil, how it loves its secret

Heath, its changeling and bewildered
    Kiss, shy on its bewildered hill,
So quietly scalded, unresolved.

And then within the cells' lucid hiddenness, the slender chromosomal strands
    Begin to drift until they touch in random places, recombinant,
Exchanging. Most cunning of storms, of boundaries altering without threat or terror,
    They seem a form of tenderness, enslaved to no right way,
No single outcome. Intent

Is a hard shelter: the gold mask over the Pharaoh's face, its smile cool
    And unchanging. But how supple the impenitent inner is
Where I can't see it, though I carry it in me—
    Where eyes are useless, and thinking, and the sun.

Suspense carries so many eclipses in it, so many edges of banishment,
   So much curve. Still, I think there is no comfort of mind but in this unmended
And self-canceling passage. My self-stung eyes lead me awkward and away.
   I can feel no *before* or *after* anymore, only how time slips back and forth
On my skin, stretching out or circling in, cryptic and unticking.
   These woods unlock plainly. Chance roughens what I am. Ransom is a hollow act.

Then I came to an edge of very calm
    But couldn't stay there. It was the washed greenblue mapmakers use to indicate
Inlets and coves, softbroken contours where the land leaves off
    And water lies plainly, as if lamped by its own justice. I hardly know how to say how it was
Though it spoke to me most kindly,
    Unlike a hard afterwards or the motions of forestalling.

Now in evening light the far-off ridge carries marks of burning.
    The hills turn thundercolored, and my thoughts move toward them, rough skins
Without their bodies. What is the part of us that feels it isn't named, that doesn't know
    How to respond to any name? That scarcely or not at all can lift its head
Into the blue and so unfold there?

Retreating figure

Always there is a retreating figure

Dry rocks, a heath, some twigs

Where authority breaks down *experiment escorts us*

Dry rocks then tempest and then rags

Ragelight and then gradually

A breaking in the mind like something lashed unlashed

The mind different then, a river lapping its banks

No longer insisting it's only plunge and tremor

The banks mossy as when softness lures and bewilders the bewildered heart

.   .   .

Always there is a retreating figure

The sky unremarkable above it

The earth radioactive or not, the power lines buzzing or not

Phones in each of the houses or phones not yet invented

Or phones already obsolete

It's hard to walk for so long year in year out but the figure walks it walks

Is it blind has it a stick has it a daughter

Somewhere the built world going on about its business

Somewhere buildings crowding ever closer

. . .

Always there is a retreating figure

(But my skin is almost nothing now, a tapestry of doubts, a tablet evanescing)

All around it the quiet bedlam of each fact

What's conclusive or not, newly proven or not

Then the conclusions contradicted, the conclusions revised or thrown away

What does it want where is it going

Its feet registering the unevenness of earth

(If there were an otherwise in me, if I could feel a clean extinction)

Bare rocks up ahead bare rocks behind it

And in its ears the heavy silence of the balance sheets, the tallies

Then the ledgers tearing

The ledgers burning free

For I have come to see I must live at some distance
    From *convinced,* from the sense of finding, being found, such rightness
As bears in upon the mind
    The way sun defines branches and leaves, singling them plainly.

In storms of mostly-over
    I am air entangling with itself, or the palm of a hand on a table lightly drawing off the dust
From something fled or buried away.
    How scarcely or not at all discernable, the ways the mind seeks to comfort itself
But doesn't govern the perplexities of shadow
    That hold it fast. I can't think of altering anything. Rough this injuring by which we learn
The might of things that strike us, and April now blossoming
    Into the rips and suddenness of silver light.

The Fifteenth Remove

Today we waded over the Banquang river, so cold.
  I remember when I used to sleep quietly without workings in my thoughts.
I know now that I am and have been a careless creature.

O Banker, Self, I feel your rigid calculations. How careful you are,
  Tallying your savings and loans, keeping track of each balance sheet and ledger.
But beneath those computations, what terror of cast-away is there
  In you, what rough disordered stricknenness and error?
What merciless rearrangement and away?

How strong it is this green, this blueness,
    And doesn't dim now but brightens,
Gathering and discharging over the troubled headland
    Of the self. Sometimes what you look at hard seems to look hard at you.
Even as the skin below my eyes gradually hollows and softens, I see glowing edges
    On the mountains that aren't stalled or lodged in struggle with the mind.
I feel wind like the tearing of cloth, and stand in the accidental strokes of this
    Disordered field, its crossings and taperings, which move through me and across me
And so knit.

And having no lodging but the cold
    We move through damage and cleanse, through the manifesting *no's*
And *sometimes gently.* These eyes, though armed with watching, seem of little power to me now,
    Like hunting empty-handed. How I'm owned by that which will not answer.
Property of _____. Inhabitant of _____. I think now it was always so.
    Torn shawl of the unsettled wraps me. Name is an odd careful and a flaw.
All the labels of me burn. Away has many layers of begin.

But if there were to be a rescue, a return, I am pluralled now, and stranger.
   What sovereignty is left in me but these brisk or delicate warrings, rogue-states
Splintering, unchaining. Storms feed on themselves, becoming their own captors
   And protectors both. Clash releases an odd tenderness.
Comfort hides its barbed *and yet*.

We cross it is so cold the first frost has fallen we rest we cook we talk continue on.

Some of these poems involve interactions with Gerard Manley Hopkins's journals, notebooks, and letters. They contain word-clusters and some sentences from those works, and a few pieces are based on incidents he recounted. Other texts drawn upon include the writings of William James and Ralph Waldo Emerson. In "Genome" the translated Greek passage is from Guy Davenport's translation of Sappho's fragment 24 in 7 *Greeks*.

The Removes series draws on American captivity narratives, while not strictly limiting itself to that context or story line. It incorporates language from those accounts, including those by Elizabeth Hanson, Nehemiah How, Mary Rowlandson, and Hannah Swarnton. The term "Remove" can be found in Mary Rowlandson's narrative: she divides her captive journey, beginning on the 10th of February 1676 and ending on April 12th of that same year, into Nineteen Removes.

The phrase "clockwork prayer" is from the artist Elizabeth King. The poem in which it appears is dedicated to her.

ACKNOWLEDGMENTS

My gratitude to the Radcliffe Institute for Advanced Study at Harvard for the Fellowship year during which I completed this book. Thanks as well to all those who read and commented on the manuscript. I am particularly grateful to Deb Garrison.

I would also like to thank the editors of the magazines in which some of these poems first appeared, sometimes in slightly different versions. All the poems, except for the Removes, originally appeared simply under the title "Poem"; they are identified here by the phrase-titles they carry in this book:

Crowd: "This green, this blueness," "Yet this may be so delicate"

Harvard Review: "Tossed-back," "No clockwork prayer," "A crisp whiteness," "And water lies plainly," "So many bending threads," "The Sixth Remove" (originally titled "Poem"), "A quiet skin," "Uncharted peace"

The Iowa Review: "But couldn't cross," "Did not foresee," "No summer as yet"

Pool: "As when red sky," "This white unswaying place"

TriQuarterly: "The First Remove," "The Second Remove," "The Fifth Remove" (originally published as "The Third Remove"), "The Seventh Remove" (originally published as "The Fourth Remove"), "The Fourteenth Remove" (originally published as "The Fifth Remove")

Verse: "September light," "Maelstroms"

The Hunterdon Museum of Art also printed [And water lies plainly] in its catalogue *Correspondences: Poetry and Contemporary Art,* to accompany the exhibit of the same name (October 12, 2003–January 4, 2004), in which this poem appeared.

A NOTE ABOUT THE AUTHOR

Laurie Sheck is the author of four previous books of poetry, including *Black Series* and *The Willow Grove,* which was a finalist for the Pulitzer Prize. Her work appears widely in such publications as *The New Yorker* and journals such as *The Kenyon Review, Verse,* and *Boston Review.* The recipient of fellowships from the Guggenheim Foundation, the National Endowment for the Arts, and the Ingram Merrill Foundation, Sheck has also been a fellow at the Radcliffe Institute for Advanced Study and is a Fellow at the Cullman Center for Scholars and Writers at the New York Public Library for 2006–7. She teaches in the MFA Program at the New School and lives in New York City.

A NOTE ON THE TYPE

This book was set in Granjon, a type named in compliment to Robert Granjon, a type cutter and printer active in Antwerp, Lyons, Rome, and Paris from 1523 to 1590. Granjon, the boldest and most original designer of his time, was one of the first to practice the trade of typefounder apart from that of printer.

Linotype Granjon was designed by George W. Jones, who based his drawings on a face used by Claude Garamond (ca. 1480–1561) in his beautiful French books. Granjon more closely resembles Garamond's own type than do any of the various modern faces that bear his name.

Composed by Stratford Publishing Services, Brattleboro, Vermont

Printed and bound by Thomson-Shore, Inc., Dexter, Michigan

Designed by Soonyoung Kwon